DIARY OF A BROKEN-HEARTED GIRL

THE NAKED TRUTH: ALL REVEALED

QUISHAUNA HAIRSTON

TO MY GRANDMOTHER IRENE "MICK" HAIRSTON. I KNOW YOU ARE LOOKING DOWN ON ME SAYING "JOB WELL DONE".

I WAS GIFTED WITH BEING A DESCENDANT OF AN UNCOMPROMISING WOMAN. IN THE NINE YEARS OF MY LIFE, I WAS ABLE TO SPEND WITH HER, I HAVE LEARNED MORE THAN MANY HAVE TRIED TO TEACH ME IN MY LIFETIME.

I WILL ALWAYS STAND FIRM ON WHO I AM. STAND FIRM ON THE CHOICES I MAKE. STAND TRUE TO MY TRUTH

NO MATTER WHO
ATTEMPTS TO JUDGE.

CONTINUE TO LIVE
THROUGH ME. CONTINUE
TO GUIDE ME. CONTINUE TO
PROTECT ME. CONTINUE TO
COVER ME IN YOUR LOVE.

OUR HAIRSTON NAME WILL
LIVE ON. THE NEGATIVITY
WILL TRANSITION INTO
POSITIVE. MY GENERATION
IS BREAKING ALL
GENERATIONAL CURSES. THE
DEMONS OF THE FAMILY
WILL NO LONGER EXIST.

All Revealed

Yeah, I know. A lot of y'all heads are still spinning from where I left off. What can I say? Other than the fact that I am not this perfect being that so many imagined me to be. I let the desire of revenge get the best of me. Sad part about it, I did not even have the opportunity to admit my wrong doings in the way I thought I would be able to. Instead, I walked away with no intentions of ever looking back.

Looking myself in the mirror daily began to destroy me. I felt an emptiness like never before. I could not take back the unthinkable but I refused to let it take away what I had left of me. I quickly learn to live with myself as if it never took place. I put it in the back of my mind praying that it would never resurface again. The only people that knew of this encounter was us, at least that's what I thought.

Four months later my life took a different turn. For the past two years I had a man that was often showing his interest in me. But that was another line that couldn't, shouldn't, and was never to be crossed. My Stockholm loves cousin was pressing me hard. Soon it became something I couldn't ignore. He was A great friend to me. We could talk for hours about any and everything. I never looked at him as more than my friend for the longest time. On my end our relationship was totally innocent. We hung out often. Went to the movies, comedy shows, or just pulled up on one another.

After a while he stopped mentioning anything involving us being anything more than friends. He began to just live in the moments of what he had with me. Being a real friend to me is all I needed from him. It was all I wanted from him. I was always overwhelmed with the number of guys who claimed to want to date me. When I was smart enough to know that many of their only interest in me stimmed from my attractiveness.

Standing at five feet and four inches, one hundred and forty pounds, hair and nails done at all times plus the bonus that I was twenty-four with no kids. I had three jobs, drove a Lexus and had my own crib. So, I was what some people would call a "Good Look" or "Hot

Commodity". Being someone's trophy has never been an interest of mine. Though it was always difficult for anyone to get my attention. Even with the poor choices I've made.

I notice how strong our friendship had grown during an all-expense paid trip to Chicago. I was I living it up with some of the world most bossed up men. Showing my homegirl and I the time of our lives. I was glad that she had invited me. That was definitely my first experience being in the company of men that had reached their financial level. I had been spoiled before but not ever on this level.

We went to amusement parks, out shopping, dined at the finest restaurant right on the water, stayed in the best hotels including the Trump and ended it staying at the Sybaris Suites. Like what twenty-four-year-old woman did I know that was staying in pool suites? Not one and I loved every moment of it. Even with all that, I wasn't impress by the money or lifestyle. It was fun for the moment, however dealing with those kinds of guys would have only left me in a situation where I'd be a statistic. I wanted more for myself. I wanted loved not expensive trips and gifts to keep me quiet. It was clear that I would be living a life of fake happiness if I stayed on that path. I left the trip without exchanging numbers with the person who made my trip unforgettable. He was a gentleman, unlike some of the other who flaunted their cockiness. Young woman or not, I knew exactly what I wanted and it didn't come with a price tag on it.

So even though I had an attractive, well-off man right in my face, every free moment I had while on the trip, I was on the phone with Cousin. During my flight home I thought to myself maybe I was missing my blessing trying to protect Stockholm's feelings. I had already secretly crossed him in the worse way. Even if it was revenge. That was the lowest anyone could go.

I arrived to the airport and got right on the phone with Cousin. He invited me to stay at his house for the night. He only stayed twenty minutes from the airport compared to the hour I would have to drive home. Without a second thought I said yes.

He greeted me with a

tight squeezed hug as always. Then walked me back to his room where he had everything ready for me to shower and prepare for bed. Even down to the shampoo I requested. Though he was being polite, I didn't look into it to be any more than that. He was always attentive to my simply needs and I always appreciated him for that.

After my shower I dressed for bed. We sat on the bed, talked, laughed, and finished up a show that was playing on tv. Good vibes per usual. I found myself restless, so I laid down right there instead of excusing myself to one of the guest rooms. I was used to sleeping next to my male friends without it being anything sexual ever happening. Us being intimate was the last thing on my mind. I laid down and said goodnight. As the night drew later, I could feel his hands making their way down my thighs. From outer thighs to my inner. I opened my eyes to look him in the face. Followed by him planting his lips upon mine.

He whispers to me, "We shouldn't be doing this". As if he didn't initiate this. Still using his hands to explore my body. I didn't say a word, as his kisses got lower and lower. He inhaled my vulva and the rest was history.

The next morning, I woke up with no regrets. I made it clear to him that in order for us to have anything real I would need to talk to my Stockholm love. I don't know why his approval was important to me, but it was necessary in order for me to move forward with Cousin. Despite his constant disrespect and somewhat feeling like I didn't owe him shit but my core beliefs was that even the most indecent person deserves to be treated fairly. He can thank my mother for that.

A few weeks had passed. Stockholm and I haven't seen

one another but he had started calling again. I know that he was only checking to see if I had moved on so he could try to suck me back in before someone had a chance with me. I just told him I needed to see him to have a face-to-face conversation. That never got the chance to happen. Cousin said he had talked to him and Stockholm said he didn't care. I must admit, I was crushed. I never thought he would ever let me go so easy. I thought to myself that what was being told to me was bullshit. Either way I had to put my thoughts in the back of my mind that what was being said was bullshit. In time the truth has always been revealed but for now I was to live in the moment.

I moved forward with what was presented to me. One night turned into two. One month became a year. A year became four. Within those four years. Friends became lovers. Lovers became a commitment. Commitment became an engagement. We had our share of ups and downs. Eventually I had to walk away.

Have I ever cheated? No. Has he? Honestly, I don't know. I've never been the type to go through phones. I can honestly say that he just didn't trust me completely with his heart. He had all the right not to do so. From day one he has always been aware of my love for

Stockholm. He was aware that I would have a love for him forever and he was willing to live with the circumstances to be with me. He shouldn't have. He deserved more than a broken female that was incapable of loving him properly.

Yes, he played a part in our breakup, but I'll speak on that another time. At the end of the day there is so much I could have done differently. In fact, he was the one who made me remember how I crossed Stockholm. He's read messages between me and Stockholm's father that he didn't delete. Years of conversations that led up to our encounter I thought would be the ultimate revenge. Instead, it haunted me throughout my relationship with cousin. He knew the entire time and finally built up the courage to ask me.

Even though the situation was meant to be buried I know that I should have given him a choice on if he still wanted to be with me under those circumstances as well. I should have trusted my gut to just tell him directly instead of listening to my one friend who encourage it to occur in the first place. He deserved the truth. From that moment of having to be faced with fact that I should have told him from my own lips, even though he knew, I made A promise that I would never do that to anyone else. I made a promise that wouldn't never allow someone do ever do that to me. I put myself in his shoes to be able to understand the thoughts in his head. He spent our entire relationship waiting on me to be straight up with him. I should have never put him in position to have to ask. I completely understand why his lack of trust in me was deeper than the love I had for Stockholm.

I was double wrong for the fact that I allowed my Stockholm love to still have access to me. He didn't have my number but I would still respond to his DM's when he would reach out. He never really disrespected our relationship. He would tell me he was happy for me. That he still loved me often but me being happy was what mattered most. I believe that for the most part. Except for when cousin and I got engaged. He would threaten to speak up at the wedding. He said a lot of crazy things at first and eventually cooled his heels.

Do I have any regret on how I handled the situation with cousin? The answer is a quick no. I had believed that he should be one to hurt from it and in many ways I did myself. Overall, we both learned from the situation. I'm pretty sure he wants me prayer for a woman he wants. Instead, he will pray for the woman God has for him. I've learned that I have to be completely done with someone before letting the next person get close to me. I learned to always tell the truth upfront no matter how ugly it is. People deserve to be able to make a choice about if they can look pass anything that may affect them emotionally.

As soon as Stockholm found out I was single again all that wishing me well went out the window. He was on me like white on rice. He started calling me daily and we would talk for hours. He was saying all the right things and or course he had giving me every reason to never trust his word. Me being me I always let go of all he ever did before that moment and was willing to give him a chance all over again. A clean slate to just fuck me over again. I tried my best to keep from repeating the cycle.

I had moved to Atlanta at this point. Soon to be twenty-eight and living my life. My life had taken a turn for the better. Stockholm would facetime me daily asking for me to be his girl again. As much as I didn't trust him, I thought about it too often to say no. I had so much hope for us to one day to get it right. I don't know why I did after so much and that had taken place. Especially without us having any intimate dealings for four years. He had to show me how much he really wanted me back.

I put him to the ultimate test. That meant it was time for me to reveal my wrong. Even with all the things he had did to me I still didn't think he deserved that level of payback. What was done was done. No taking it back. Now I was to speak on once again a memory I tried to erase for so many years.

I told him that if we were going to try again there was something I needed to tell him. He said, "What you fucked somebody?". I said yes as tears started running uncontrollable down my face. He took his time guessing names and finally said, "My daddy". I said yes again only to end up crying harder. I thought to myself there was no way he was going to still want to be with me after that. I was wrong. He screamed at me, "Wipe them motherfucking tears off your face, you know I hate seeing you cry. I don't care about none of that. I still love you and you still gone be my wife one day". I wiped away my tears as he said, "This ain't the first time he has done this to me. What's fucked up about you is that he knows how I feel about you".

Now that the air was cleared, we were back like we never had time apart. When I went to my hometown to visit, we would hang out and talk about all the things we overcame. I couldn't help but to pay attention to the fact that there were more bad memories than good ones. There was no way I could forget that we use to have fist fights. There was no way I could forget how cold he would act towards me at times. More importantly there was no way I could forget all the other women. I chose to forgive him though just as he had forgiven me. I let the past be just that. Like all the times before. We were moving forward with no looking back.

It took a while before the opportunity presented itself for us to take things further. I just so happen to come in town around his birthday and he asked to spend it with me. I pulled up on him for a little bit and told him to enjoy his night with his friends and I'll see him later. The plan was to go to club after his kickback. He wasn't with that. Just like always he curved his friends and the club because he would just rather be with me. I felt young again. One thing

I could say is I always came before time with the homies and the club any day.

    We entered the house where I was staying for the weekend. Watched movies, talked, and relaxed. He looked at me and said, "We have all night, no need to rush". My heart melted. I giggled on the inside because I could still see that he still got nervous around me after all these years. I noticed that about him years ago, when I stopped looking at his hard shell and focused on his body language.

I started to get tired. I turned to face him to lay in his arms. He kissed me softly on my forehead and ask to see my phone. He turned on some music and began to make love to me. He grabbed my phone again to recorded himself tasting me. When he put it back down, he said he wanted me to watch it every time I missed him. We kept going over and over until we were both out of energy. He held me throughout the night just like old times. I just lived in the moment because deep down inside I knew who I was dealing with. A special moment could turn into a moment of sorrow in the blink of an eye.

The morning after I dropped him off and returned to Atlanta to get back to the reality of what things really were. I had heard he was dating someone on and off. After about a month I found that to be true when the communication with us had just about ceased. Except for his regular monthly call. He would make to tell me he loves me. I'm sure he did that to see if I was still stupid. Sadly, he was right.

Two months had passed and I still had no period. I was thinking to myself, "Hell no, not again, not now". I took so many pregnancies test I lost count. One came back positive but was soon determined to be a faulty test because the one that followed was negative. To clear my head, I made an appointment with the doctor immediately to be extra sure I was NEGATIVE!!!! The biggest concern was why I wasn't getting a cycle. I decided to have a series of test ran and had to wait a week for my results.

Once I got that call to come into the office, I didn't know what I was about to hear. She let me know that all my STD results were negative and that her concern was my hormone test. An average woman has a hormone level of fifty. My hormone level was an eight. To explain what that meant, she drew out charts as she made it clear to me that I would never conceive naturally. I heard her clearly but I was still unable to process what had been said to me. I called my mother to let her know the news. As I said the words out loud myself, reality hit me. In my mind I was to blame for this. In my mind God took my ability to become a mother because I took it for granted. I didn't question him. I felt like God had all the right to do so. I sacrificed my only child years ago and I would have to live with that decision for the rest of my life.

I couldn't sit around and feel bad for myself. Life went on as always and I couldn't move forward if I was still looking back. I had to let go of everything that kept me bound. I took some much-needed time for myself. I stopped communicating with my Stockholm love before I even got my results because once again, he was being an ass. He was entertaining too many and I was a too far away to allow mistreatment from a distance.

It's now my second year living in Atlanta. I stay clear from dating to take time to just focus on me. I desperately needed to find myself. I did just that. I had time to figure out what made me happy. I spent a lot of time working but I always made free time for my girls. I had to remove the thoughts of how much I wanted someone to love me and learn how to love myself properly.

My career as a traveling hair stylist had picked up tremendously and I was always booked up and flying to new locations almost every week. I would have to leave home for several weeks at a time on some occasions. I was living my best life. Out on my own. It felt so good. I had found a level of peace that I never could imagine. I needed this peace more than any fake love some man could give me.

I was stopped in my tracks and the love bug bit me again. I met this extraordinary guy through my family. When I say extraordinary, I mean just that. He was extra but no one kept me smiling the way he did. That man catered to my every need without me even needing to ask. He just did. We grew close really fast. So fast that when I could come home off the road, I would go straight to him.

He had a career of his own that required him to travel as well. We began to plan our travels around the same time so we could come home together. It was a beautiful moment that was short lived as soon as I found out he was being dishonest with me. Karma had come around for me. The same way

I withheld information from my ex-fiancé. Information had been withheld from me. It didn't feel good but I chucked it up and moved on with my life with no hard feelings towards him. I understood what it was like to fall for someone unexpectedly. Trying to battle with the truth and what was wanted in the end.

We parted ways that August. I was packed and made my way to start a new journey in Texas. Texas was always the place I wanted to live. I was just waiting on the timing to be right and once it was, I took off. Opportunities opened up for me quickly. I established a place to call home in the middle of constantly traveling state to state servicing my clients.

I had been there a few months and boom! I receive one of those faithful calls that was sure to come. I didn't know the number, so I hesitated on answering the facetime. I decided to pick up and all I could see was Stockholm's smiling face all in the camera. I hung up immediately. I wasn't having it. I couldn't allow my kryptonite access to me again. It was a losing battle every time.

I spent way too much time trying to break the chain with this man. I needed for this nightmare to be over already but it was far from over. He called me over and over again until I picked up for him again. "What do you want?", I said as furious as I could. "Baby you know I love you. I just need to see your face. You still living in Atlanta or you moved back home". "I live in Texas", I replied. The conversation continued for hours. Yes, hours. No matter how much I needed to fight it, I still had a soft spot for him and he knew how to use it to his advantage.

What saved me was the fact I was half way across the country, so his advances for us to get back together went in one ear and out the other. Especially when he mentioned him coming to move to Texas with me. One thing I wasn't with was that. All he was gone do was come out there to cheat with new bitches. Ain't no way I was going out like that. Plus allowing a man to live with me went against everything I always believed in. I didn't allow him to move in my first apartment, so no way I was doing it half way across the country.

I know he was only calling cause him and his girl had broken up. I knew that was temporary. She was just too beneficial to his life and the shit she does for him I would never do. He knew in order to be with me at this point in my life it would require him to be a man and that's not something I could ever see him being ready for.

He wore his immaturity well. I was good on not

having a man that could provide for me in the ways that I had made myself accustom to.

I took advantage of the conversation because I needed his permission to tell our story if I decided to use names. He said yes but of course he probably thought I was only going to talk about the fairytale parts that we were living. Nope he was wrong. Yes, we had so many great memories together. But if I put my focus on all the good things, chances are he would have sucked me back into his world again. I'm just being honest. When things were good, I was always on clouds.

He's always spoken greatness into my life. Always spoke on how he knew that I was going to be somebody big and do great things. It's like he knew who I was born to be before I did. I can say that he did motivate me in all my success but fuck all that. He was an addiction that I had to wing myself off of.

I had been living in Texas for a year by this time. I often traveled to my hometown but I never allowed him to see me. I don't know why I allowed it this time. I mean really, I was thirty at this point. I should have learned my lesson by now. It was up to me to break the cycle but yet again I dropped the ball.

He pulled up at my fathers to see me. My dad was so happy to see him but I don't know the fuck why. He was happier to see him than I was. My dad even mentioned to us that we should get back together so we can have him some grandchildren. Stockholm sucked up all the hype. The whole time I'm thinking, "HEEEEELLLLLLLL NNNNOOOO". We talked for a while and I sent him on his way after making sure he put some money in my hands of course. He was living it up and I felt like I deserve every bit of it for all the time we wasted.

The next day he reached out to me and asked if I could do his hair because he was growing it out. I laughed inside because I knew it was a tack tick to see me again. I said yes because I was definitely going to take his money once again. When he arrived, I was still in the middle of coloring my own hair. I had recently cut it all off and was trying a new look.

He offered to shampoo it for me. I let him. We talked and laughed as he actually did a good job with shampooing my hair. He towel dried it for me and I made my way to the coach for a moment get the blood to come down that had rushed to my head. I was startled immediately by him. I didn't realize that he was right behind me and met my lap with his face as soon as I sat down.

I didn't even have a moment to gather my thoughts. He had lifted my dress and was face deep between my thighs before I could even catch my breath. It felt so good no way I was stopping him. Even though my thoughts told me to. One thing led to another and moments after it was over.

We talk as I actually did his hair right after and he said he hopes that I get pregnant because he wanted his family back. I explained to him for the hundredth time that I wasn't even capable of conceiving naturally. He started asking how much it would cost and what I'd have to do to make it happen. As if we haven't already had this conversation from the first moment we spoke again after I got the news from my doctor. In my head I knew God wasn't going to allow him to have that opportunity again.

Did I tell you that I felt nothing? Usually after our

encounters, I be stuck back to him like glue. This time was different. I felt absolutely no emotional feeling to him. I think that he could feel my disconnection that I had from him by my actions and choice of words.

Later that evening as I rested alone, I thought back over that actions that had took place. I had to ask myself what had changed. It became apparent to me what it was. I had forgiven myself for allowing myself to go through things with anyone that I didn't have to go through. I forgave myself for being the reason I lost my child. I forgave myself for all the years I spent not loving me. I had forgiven myself for inflicting any pain on myself.

I was finally free from what kept me bound to my Stockholm lover. If I knew all it would take was for me to forgive myself, I would have worked on that before I gave fourteen years of my life away. I know that the pain was necessary. I know that every mistake that I've made with love was necessary. I know with the mistakes I've made with not being honest with myself was necessary.

The truth cannot be buried. Facing my truth was the best thing I could of did for me. Facing my truth help me begin my journey of healing. I had to stop caring about what anyone would think of me and own my shit.

All Revealed

The biggest issue that most people have is forgiving themselves. I had not forgiven myself for the loss of our child. It was 100% my fault despite any hurtful things that he said to me. I had a choice, and my choice was to make a poor decision that would affect me until I stop giving it power.

He was able to use my downfall to his advantage by telling me constantly that I owed him a child. I spent so many years trying to right my wrong and give him the child that I took from him. I carried this on my heart for so many years. But I also know that this situation was with purpose.

He was the reason that I was forced to learn to love myself and put myself first. The blessing of learning to love self is a battle that many fight. There are many who are older than me and still don't know how to love themselves. It is one of the biggest battles that many have to face daily.

He taught me the importance of loyalty. You never want someone that close to you that you cannot trust with your feelings. A broken heart could kill you. Is having someone that's disloyal around you worth dying for?

He taught me the meaning of loving unconditionally. We loved one another without condition. The love we had was not based on the fact that it was beneficial. It was developed without reason. That's why I never loved him any less based on his flaws and he loved me despite my acts of retaliation.

He taught me that the best revenge is no revenge. Simply move on and let God handle your battles. We should never lower ourselves to respond to the actions of others.

He taught me that life is what you make it. I made the choice to be in this situation with him. I wanted more for myself but countless times I chose him. When I finally chose me, my life changed overnight. Life was always better without him but once I made the choice to never look back, the transitions of my life reached new levels.

He taught me the value of love and how it is never to be misused. I will never take advantage of the love that someone has for me. If I can't love them properly, I refuse to be selfish and try to hold on to it when someone else is deserving of it.

All Revealed

But wait there's
more!!!!!!!!!!!

One of the biggest things that takes place daily is a grown ass man preying on a young girls. As far back as being the age of seven, I could remember feeling uneasy because I could feel the energy of a man having an attraction for me. I have countless untold stories of different men that I've encountered that have told me straight up that they waited for me to turn eighteen so they could have dealings with me. This is more common than people speak of. Even with having little crushes on grown men as I got older. The feeling was evident to be mutual. If I was fast enough to act on it, they would have engaged in the interaction. I am lucky enough to say that no one has ever tried to take my innocents but waiting to manipulate my mind is just as bad.

Young women seem to think that it's cute when an older man has interest in them. I strongly feel that a young woman in the age range up to twenty-five, are in the years of finding herself. During these years if she is dating, it's more likely that she will mold into the woman that the man she is dating wants her to be. She becomes lost in him.

She walks the ways he wants her to walk. Talks the way he wants her to talk. Dresses the way he prefers for her to dress. Thinks the way he wants her to think. I'm not saying all women but many. Especially those who have an absence of a parent or both and is in search of love or acceptance. Becoming an individual and knowing who she is at the end of the day is less likely.

Some will break from this spell but many will not. For

those that do, it takes her years to first restore a mental balance. It takes years of to understand her value. It takes her years to know what she wants for herself.

We must invest more time in becoming better role models for our young women. They are always watching. I'll never make excuses for the choices I've made but I know a lot of the things I've witness growing up either made me curious or

turned me away from doing
the same.

FIND YOUR PEACE!!!!

Please take a moment to reflect on your own life story. STOP being so hard on yourself. All poor choices develop great people. I will say that life is the greatest teacher a million times. We never know what's best for us if we never know what wrong for us. Embrace the things that you were once shameful of. Speak your truth. Fuck anyone who still feels the need to judge others as if they are imperfect people. Learn to love you more than you can even love another. Forgive yourself!!!! And move forward. Create your own destiny, don't allow anyone to write your life story. You can always rewrite the ending when you put your life in your hands and not of those who only want to keep you

down. The time is now!!!!

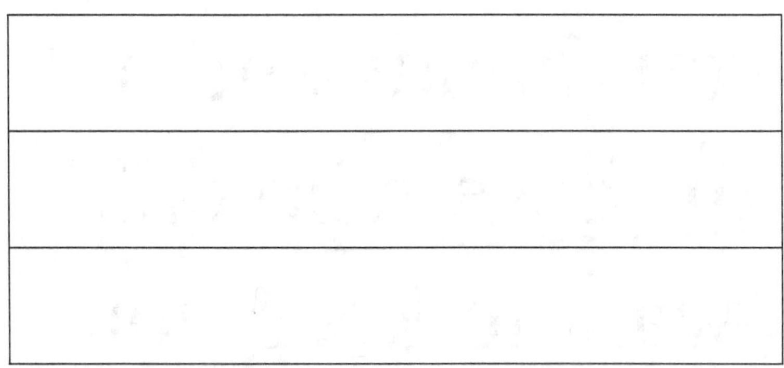

91
All Revealed

All Revealed

95
All Revealed

All Revealed

97